Tex-tiles and other

Using Medieval tiles and stonework

Yvonne Brown

First thoughts

Medieval Tiles in Blue (left) and detail (below) — Yvonne Brown

Yes I know medieval tiles are never blue, but a little artistic licence never hurts!

The on-point layout in this piece makes for a more dynamic design – the juxtaposition of the darker tile panel with the plain, densely quilted 'tiles' provides a neat contrast and creates a frame. The geometric tiles are strip-pieced squares, again heavily quilted to create texture. Note the 'broken' edges where the tiles have worn!

I have always been a 'maker', someone with a compulsion to dabble in the world of arts and crafts. I love to record the world around me through painting, drawing and photography – and then to use that collected information as source material for my artwork.

Much of that work will end up as a textile piece.

Even as a young girl I found fabric fascinating. I love the richness of its surfaces and its tactile qualities, whether it is used for clothing and soft furnishings or for the less functional items that I so enjoy producing. Although I have had little formal art training, good fortune has allowed me some involvement in the world of art. As a City & Guilds embroidery student I have had the freedom to experiment with a huge variety of textile techniques – and gained skills which have helped me translate my ideas into tangible form.

Studying the History of Art and Architecture at the University of East Anglia as a mature student opened my eyes and mind to a whole new world, and gave me the confidence to pursue my interests with enthusiasm. Through this course I came to a better understanding of the art of the past, and gained a greater appreciation of the creative imagination and remarkable skills of past masters.

I studied Medieval art and architecture in particular depth, and discovered an enduring passion for all things medieval, from the architecture and stonework of mighty cathedrals and abbeys to the exquisite artefacts made by master craftsmen and the decorated books produced in monasteries and scriptoria all across Europe.

I am curious about their origins, and the audacity of makers and patrons who could commission such wonderful work at a time when tools and materials were so rudimentary. And I marvel at the sophistication and intricacy of designs that have influenced so much of our culture and heritage.

Of course, there is a spirituality and mysticism attached to all these things which has become romanticised over the passage of time – ideas that reached their most complete fulfilment in the Arts and Crafts movement. In their eyes this was to be an ideal time of honest craftsmanship and beautiful design.

It is a view I share, though I do feel the need to go deeper. I have a need to analyse what is so attractive about all these objects, and what precisely I am seeing when I use medieval designs as inspiration for my own work. I look at shapes, colours, patterns and textures. I look at the history of the objects. And I look at the many ways in which the passage of time has changed them, and in particular their surface, which may be weathered, worn, corroded or tarnished.

As a textile artist, how can I encapsulate the excitement I feel for the object in a textile piece? How can I show others what I find so fascinating about its shape, its colour or its texture? And how can I use my own knowledge, skills and techniques to the best possible effect?

In this book I hope to show you how I have been influenced by particular images and objects – and then to take you through the processes I have used to create textile pieces based on those sources.

Developing and refining those processes has been a long and fascinating journey.

After trying many ways to achieve the appearance of an aged and distressed surface I discovered that melting and burning synthetics with heat tools was not only great fun, but created exactly the appearance I was looking for.

Synthetic fabrics, especially voiles and organzas, react very well to being cut with a soldering iron or zapped with a heat gun, especially after they have been stitched to a natural fibre base. Even so, the results are still some way from resembling the worn tiles and sculpture that were inspiring me.

My eureka moment came when I discovered synthetic felt. Acrylic felt will cut quickly and cleanly with the soldering iron, but resists being melted with the heat gun. Kunin felt, however, reacts quickly and dramatically. When zapped with the heat gun the surface 'honeycombs' to create an immediate textured surface with a slight plasticity that can easily be painted or coloured with a variety of colouring agents.

The felt is available in a variety of colours, but none resembles the soft shades found in the worn medieval tiles I was looking at. More experiments followed so further experiments led me to colour white felt with a soft wash of transfer paints, being synthetic the felt will take these disperse dyes well and by painting them first on to paper it is easy to create a light, abstract wash of colour.

All I needed to do now was to work out how to use these materials to translate my ideas into my finished art work.

Recreating the medieval tile using transfer dyed felt which can be further trimmed and distressed using heat tools

Materials and skills to acquire:

- Heat sensitive felt
- Transfer dyes
- Accurate sewing of tile inlay shapes using reverse techniques
- Cutting sewn shapes using a soldering iron
- Honeycombing using a heat gun
- Painting and collaging skills

Tiles from Winchester Cathedral (W) and
from the ruined monasteries of Byland (B)
and Rievaulx (R) in North Yorkshire

Medieval Tiles as a design source

The design possibilities provided by a tiled floor are infinite. It presents us with a patchwork quilt beneath our feet – a quilt already designed to perfection by someone else! We only need to select the shapes, patterns and colours we like and put them all together.

When you come across a real medieval tiled floor, or a fragment found in some ruins, the tiles will have other qualities to inspire your textile work. Often they have taken on unusual colours after absorbing the pollution and footfall of centuries. They may be encrusted with detritus, or covered in moss or lichen. Or they may be broken and cracked. These are all elements to inspire the artist and make us think of ways to develop a textured surface in fabric and stitch.

Examples of medieval tiles traced and ready to use

The development and manufacture of the various types of medieval tile happened at differing rates over a period of time. Around the British Isles there are examples of relief, line impressed, two-colour inlaid and geometric mosaic tiles dating from Anglo-Saxon times, and by the fourteenth century all the main techniques for making decorative tiles were available to the craftsman.

There are excellent examples of early geometric mosaic tiles at the Cistercian abbeys of Fountains, Byland, Rievaulx and Meaux in Yorkshire, and at Prior Crauden's Chapel in Ely Cathedral. You will also find a wonderful selection of inlaid tiles at Winchester Cathedral, in the cloisters of Muchelney Abbey, Somerset, on the refectory pavement at Cleeve Abbey and in the Chapter House of Westminster Abbey – just a few of many sites around the country waiting for you to discover them.

Synthetic Felt

After experimenting with several techniques I found that I could exploit the unique qualities of synthetic felt to produce a textured surface that looked worn and distressed, a perfect way to replicate the tiles and fragments in my source pictures.

Kunin felt made from re-cycled plastic bottles fits the bill. It is completely synthetic and will cut easily with a fine tipped soldering iron I also need it to 'honeycomb' when it is zapped with a heat gun to give a really distressed surface.

Always check your materials

It is really important to check each new batch of felt to make sure it will cut with the soldering iron and honeycomb when subjected to the heat gun.

Extra note
Can't get a felt that melts and honeycombs? Try using a firm needle-punched polyester wadding. Do a test piece first but I think you will be amazed at the results!

Colouring the felt

The felt comes in a huge range of colours, but they are all quite solid. To create the softer look I want for my tile designs, and to replicate the weathered and worn feel of the originals, I colour the felt with transfer paints. They work well on synthetics and are probably a safer option than other colouring agents when you are also using a heat tool.

What do you need?

- White Synthetic Felt
- Transfer or Disperse dyes
- Smooth, non-absorbent paper (fine cartridge or layout paper)
- Small jars or plastic pots
- Paint brushes
- Iron

Transfer or disperse dyes

Transfer or disperse dyes come ready mixed or in powder form. Powders are probably more economical, and easy to mix in varying strengths. Success often involves some trial and error, so it is wise to make notes of your experiments!

Powder dyes can be used on all types of synthetic fabrics. You will achieve softer effects on polyester, and on natural fibres you will get best results with Miracle Fix Liquid. Transfer dyes can also be thickened and used for printing.

Transfer or disperse dyes are available in a variety of colours

Using Transfer Dyes

This is not an exact science, so do experiment to achieve the results you are looking for. Mix approximately ½ tsp powder with a few drops of warm water in a small jar or plastic container, then dilute. Mark your colour pots, as they can be difficult to distinguish in liquid form. The true colours will not be apparent until you iron them off on to the fabric.

For a soft abstract effect I paint a wash of clean water on to smooth, non-absorbent paper, fine cartridge paper or layout paper, and then add the liquid transfer paints in large blobs and allow the colours to travel into each other. When the paint is dry you can iron it on to the felt. It is best to use a traditional dry iron; if you use a steam iron, even on a dry setting, you may still get imprints of the steam holes if you don't move the iron quickly enough.

To transfer the colour you will need a constant hot iron, moved very slowly over the back of the paper until the colour is activated. Just be careful, though: too much heat concentrated in one place may melt the felt and make it stick to the paper – *not* what you are aiming for! You should be able to get four or five prints of varying strengths from each painted paper.

Painting the diluted discharge dyes onto the paper

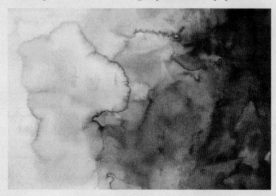
Apply the paint to wetted paper for a softer effect

Several examples of transfer painted papers

Ironing the printed paper face down to print the felt

Note: it is sensible to protect the surface of your ironing board. Have baking parchment handy in case you need to protect the felt from direct contact with the iron.

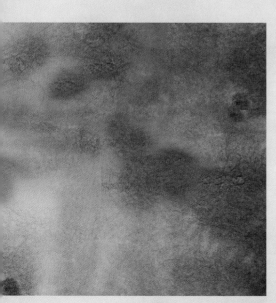
An example of transfer printed felt

Making your tiles

The technique I use to make the tiles is essentially a form of reverse appliqué, where the design is placed and sewn on the reverse side of materials. I find this a really foolproof way to get your designs on to your work, but you do need to be quite proficient with your free machining to transfer the design successfully.

What do you need?

- Background fabric: this should be a natural fibre (cotton is probably best). Choose something like a batik with a mottled look, avoiding definite prints
- Fine sew-in Vilene or Stitch and Tear
- Synthetic Felt

- A machine embroidery thread to work with your colour scheme (this should match your felt, not your background fabric). I generally use a silky rayon Madeira thread in a soft grey or neutral.
- Your design
- Your sewing machine, set up for free-machine work with a darning foot.
- A soldering iron with a very fine tip
- A heat gun
- A fine pencil or waterproof pen

Make your 'sandwich' with Vilene at the back, fabric in the middle and felt on top (coloured side facing you) and pin all four corners. You are going to turn the work over and machine from the back: this avoids the risk of any nasty accidents when you can't see the felt.

Set your machine up for free-machine work, with the feed dogs down and a darning foot. Fill the bobbin with silky rayon machine embroidery thread, and use a bobbin fil on the top of the

For this project I am working on finished 4-inch squares – but because there may be some distortion when using the heat gun, cut your background fabric into 5-inch squares. The size can be adjusted later. Cut your felt and Vilene into 4-inch squares.

Transfer your design to the Vilene using a pencil or waterproof pen; remember you will get a mirror image on the front of your work.

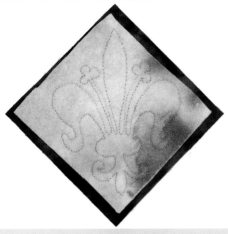

machine. Carefully machine along all the drawn lines of your design. You will get a better result if you can do this twice, but if it really is too stressful to hit that line a second time just do it once. The technique will work just as well.

Once you have machined in your design you are ready for the fun bit: cutting out with a soldering iron.

Referring to the design at all times, carefully cut away the felt that is not required, using your soldering iron. Keep the iron as upright as possible so you are only using the tip. You will not need to apply any pressure: the felt will melt quite quickly, allowing you to move the excess away with your other hand. You can tidy up any rough edges with the tip of the soldering iron afterwards; don't

Setting up your soldering iron

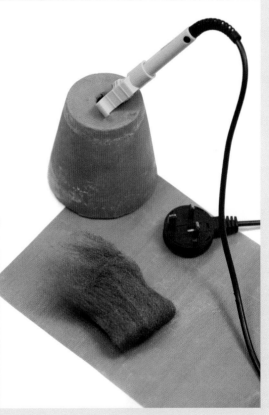

- Work on a protected surface: I use a piece of glass with bevelled edges or a piece of Bake-O-Glide from the kitchen shop.
- Support your soldering iron safely in an upturned terracotta pot
- Work in a well ventilated room and wear a mask to protect you from toxic fumes
- Keep some steel wool handy to clean the tip of your soldering iron

overwork, or you will end up with messy melted edges. Finally carefully blast the surface of the felt with the heat gun to give it a distressed look. Take care doing this – as soon as the felt starts to melt it will disappear very quickly!

Once you have made your tiles they will need a bit of a steam press on the reverse to flatten them out. Then square them up, ready to complete your patchwork piece.

Completing your tiles

T he tiles can be incorporated with a variety of patchwork blocks. So now may be the time to look at the floor pictures for inspiration!

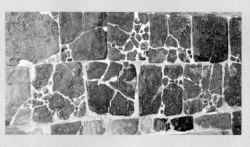

You may like to make some tiles look as if they have broken edges. To achieve this effect, lay your completed design on a larger piece of contrasting fabric in your grouting colour, and free-machine around the edge using a jeans or top-stitch thread which is slightly thicker than normal. You will need to use a top-stitch needle with a large eye. As you stitch, meander in and out, particularly at seam or tile joins. This is where the tiles would have worn naturally. Once you have completed the stitching, use a pair of small, sharp scissors and carefully cut back the tile fabric as close to the stitching as you can. Beware – try not to cut the 'grouting' fabric underneath!

Leave about 1½ inches of grouting fabric beyond the tiles and then make sure your work is square and ready to attach a border, check that the finished dimensions are compatible to the border you have chosen to construct. For example, on the small piece illustrated, my grouting fabric was squared up to 10½ inches so once my border was attached it would end up as a 10-inch square. My half square triangles are all 2 inches square, so they easily fit around the block without much effort required in the calculations.

Once your quilt top is finished, make up your quilt sandwich, pin or tack through all thicknesses and quilt either by hand or machine. Finally add a binding, and don't forget your label.

Making Half-Square Triangles

For a 2 inch finished square cut two $2^7/_8$ inch squares of contrasting fabric.

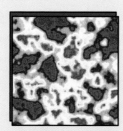

Draw a diagonal line on the back of one of the squares, from top left corner to bottom right corner and place the squares on top of each other, right sides facing.

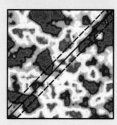

Machine ¼ inch either side of the drawn line then cut through all thicknesses on the drawn line.

You will now have two squares made up of half-square triangles. Press the seam towards the darker fabric.

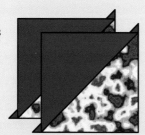

Tiles from Winchester and elsewhere and the quilts they inspired

Moving on – Stone Story:

Medieval sculpture and ancient stonework as source material

'In the Middle Ages men had no great thought that they did not write down in stone.'

Victor Hugo

.

In medieval times people did not have access to the vast array of visual stimuli that is available to us today. However, they could read the stories captured for them in the early church carvings produced with great dignity and simplicity by anonymous sculptors. These 'stone stories' are not just religious homilies. They cover the whole range of medieval life with carvings of everyday activities, the labours of the months, random creatures, monsters and fantastic foliage.

One example of a full range of early medieval sculpture can be found around the Prior's door at Ely Cathedral. Here the stunning series of sculpted arches have been open to the elements for hundreds of years, and much of the fine detail has been lost as the stone has been weathered and distressed. These stone carvings fascinate me on several levels; I am interested in their form and content but also, with an artist's eye, I am captivated and inspired by their colour, shapes and patterns, and most of all by their surface qualities. How could I use this most intriguing of source material and translate it into fabric and stitch?

Making a Stone Story panel

Stone Story 1

The process of constructing the Stone Story panels is really an extension of the tile technique. Here I have been using a combination of cut and melted synthetic felt together with a collage of found textured pieces, stitched onto a firm background support. The whole piece is then painted with gesso and acrylic paints before finishing with surface decoration and stitch.

What do you need?

- 100% cotton interlining (also known as bump)
- PVA Glue
- White synthetic felt
- Fine sew-in Vilene or Stitch and Tear
- White cotton thread
- Acrylic gesso
- A selection of acrylic paints

Before you begin, the cotton interlining (which is your base fabric) needs to be soaked in a weak solution of PVA and water, approximately 50ml of PVA to a litre of water, allow to drip dry. This should stiffen the interlining enough to support the collage.

Using designs taken from motifs in the sculpture, first trace the design onto the Vilene using a pencil or waterproof pen; bear in mind that when looking at the original sculpture some parts may have worn away, or be quite indistinct, so you may choose to fragment your design in some way to emphasise this.

Like the tiles, the design will go on the back of the interlining support. Remember you will get a mirror image on the front of your work!

Place the synthetic felt on the front of the interlining, matching it with the position of the design on the back. Don't forget to pin all four corners.

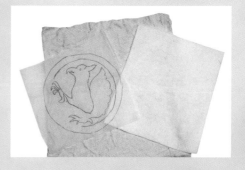

Set up your sewing machine for free-machine work with the feed dogs down and using a darning foot. Thread the machine with white cotton thread and stitch on all the drawn lines of the design. Your design will now be visible in stitch on the front of the work.

Using a fine-tipped soldering iron, and referring back to your original design, carefully cut away the felt you do not need. This will reveal the design. Once this has been done you can distress the surface of the felt with a heat gun, taking care not to melt away too much of the felt but at the same time achieving a honeycomb look on the surface.

Make a collection of found textile pieces, net, lace scrim, scrunched tissue paper, tyvek, string and cords. Try to keep these as white or neutral colours.

Still using the machine in free-machine mode, and using a straight or a zigzag stitch to couch down your pieces, build up a collage around the felt design. Don't be too precious about your stitching – use a free 'anchoring and dragging' sewing style.

Try to cover all, or most, of the background without making it look too 'busy'. Have some quieter areas just covered with net and secured with random free-machine zigzag. Even your stitches will show through once it has been flooded with paint.

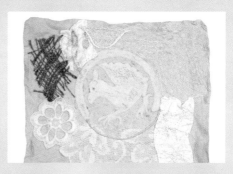

When you are happy with the density of the textured collage paint the whole panel with white acrylic gesso, taking care not to apply it too thickly as this will obliterate the textured surface. Stipple the gesso into small areas and through lace and net, making sure that all surfaces are covered. Leave to dry thoroughly.

Now you are able to paint the whole collage to suit your project. I use watered down acrylic paints; the Golden range has a wonderful strength of pigment and a full range of colours, but do experiment with alternatives.

To begin with, keep the colours very pale. I just give the surface a wash of colour which is almost like 'dirty dishwater'. Next I usually do a wash of pale yellow or ochre, as this will shine through whatever colour scheme you decide on and will highlight any elements you choose to leave exposed and not covered by a second coat.

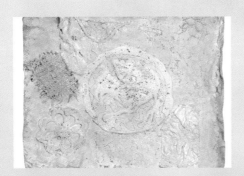

Slowly introduce your colour in transparent layers of washes – take care not to go straight in with very strong colour as it will be difficult to blend and will probably give you too strident a result.

I find that a soft wash of Payne's grey is great for knocking back areas that have become too bright.

Note: Don't panic if your colour goes all wrong! Just allow it to dry, overpaint with gesso and start again.

Once the collage is completely dry it is still possible to further enhance the surface with stitch, although machining is probably easier than hand stitch at this stage.

If you feel your piece needs to be further aged or distressed it can be lightly rubbed over with a coloured wax such as Treasure Gold, which comes in a full range of colours, not all overtly metallic. Alternatively you could use Aqua wax.

Stone Story II

Ely-Stone Story III

Small dragon and griffin based on tiles from Winchester

Examples of the Stone Story technique. Gesso is applied to the textile collage and when it is dry you can overpaint it with layers of transparent washes of acrylic paint — the colour choice is yours.

Completing & Finishing

Your finished textile collages can be mounted and framed to make small pictures. Or they can be incorporated into larger textile pieces as inserts and panels. The collages will be quite stiff but it is still possible to machine through them to complete your piece work. Complement your collage with a contrasting border. For example, this could be machine trapunto echoing the sculpture around a medieval door as in Stone Story I or a border of repeated Romanesque arches and in Ely-Stone Story III.

Examples of borders added to the textile collages

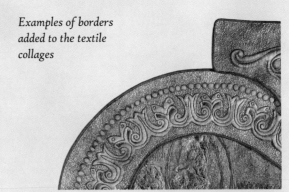

Using your imagination

Think of other subjects that could be used as your inspiration – this technique certainly doesn't have to be confined to sculpture and stonework. In the piece 'Crossword' below, I used this technique and created the letters from synthetic felt with a collage of string and lace for the background

But what about looking at corroded and rusted metal objects and structures, carved wood and drift wood, layers of rock and twisted strata. You can take inspiration from the seashore – sand, pebbles, the forests – tree bark, lichen, fungi? The list is endless!

SeaFoam is a textured sampler – lace, net, scrim and string create a rhythm of textures and colour evocative of the seashore

References

Medieval Tiles, Hans van Lemmen, Shire Books, 2004

Medieval Tile Designs, J G Nichols [ed], Dover Pictorial Archive, 1998

Transfer to Transform   Jan Beaney & Jean Littlejohn Double Trouble Enterprises, 1999

Tools

Heat tools

The fine tipped soldering iron, made by Antex is a CS18. It is 18 watts and new tips can be purchased separately. It can also be obtained with suitable plugs for different countries. It is available from a number of suppliers.
www.antex.co.uk

The heat gun is a craft model and concentrates the heat to where it will be most effective for instant results but is not as fierce as a paint stripper. There are a number of these available, make sure the one you purchase is at least 300 watts.

Suppliers

Art materials, dyes, heat tools

Art Van Go
The Studios
1 Stevenage Road,
Knebworth
Herts SG3 6AN

Tel : +44 (0) 1438 814946

Email: art@artvango.co.uk

www.artvango.co.uk

Art materials, dyes, bespoke fabric packs, Kunin Felt

Ivy House Studio
(mail order and visits be pre-arrangement only)
37 High Street
Kessingland
Suffolk NR33 7QQ

Tel: +44 (0) 1502 740414

Email: ivyhousestudio@hotmail.com

Fabrics for dyeing, interlining

Whaleys (Bradford) Ltd
Harris Court
Great Horton
Bradford
West Yorkshire BD7 4EQ

Telephone: +44 (0) 1274 576718

Email: info@whaleysltd.co.uk

www.whaleys-bradford.ltd.uk

Kunin Felt

Fashion Futures Ltd
Unit 1,
Mace Industrial Estate
Ashford

Kent TN24 8EP

Tel +44 (0) 1233 625228 and 625227

Email: fashion.futures@btconnect.com

To whet your appetite, here are some examples of the Celtic cutwork which will form the subject of my next book.

You will learn how to use heat tools and synthetic fabrics, including jewel-like gauzes, to enhance and illuminate your textile projects.

Taking inspiration from metalwork, manuscripts and carvings and using modern skills and fabrics to produce exquisite, gem-like pieces.

Hoo's treasure 1, red silk with a detail of the cutwork